Plum Island to Palm Beach
Our Sinking Shoreline

Table of Contents

Notes About This Book- 4

Acknowledgements- 5

Introduction One Lousy Birthday Present, June 1, 2017- 6

Chapter 1 The 2017 Hurricane Season- 10

Chapter 2 The Boat Wreck, Plum Island, Massachusetts- 14

Chapter 3 Plum Island- 16

Chapter 4 At A Horseshoe Crab Orgy, Pleasant Bay- 20

Chapter 5 The Jackson Lab, Durham, NH- 24

Chapter 6 The Devil Wears Pinstripes, Plum Island- 28

Chapter 7 Donald and The Iceberg- 30

Chapter 8 Dual Wing Bars, Plum Island Point- 34

Chapter 9 Reflections on Erosion, Thacher Island- 38

Chapter 10 "The Long Island Express"- 42

Chapter 11 Muskegat Island- 48

Chapter 12 The Silver Lining, Fire Island- 52

Chapter 13 Hurricane Sandy, Oceanside, Long Island- 58

CHAPTER 14 Staten Island- 62

CHAPTER 15 Sandy Hook- 66

CHAPTER 16 Bay Head, New Jersey- 72

CHAPTER 17 The Longest Night, Lavallette, New Jersey- 78

CHAPTER 18 Recover or Retreat? Tom's River, NJ- 86

CHAPTER 19 Oregon Inlet, North Carolina- 92

CHAPTER 20 New Shelly Island, Cape Hatteras, NC- 96

CHAPTER 21 Daufuskie Island, South Carolina- 100

CHAPTER 22 Cayo Costa, Florida- 104

CHAPTER 23 Lake Okeechobee- 108

CHAPTER 24 Mar-a-Lago- 112

Notes about this book

This book is written to coincide with Hurricane Sandy's Fifth Anniversary. However it covers several separate trips I took down the coast during those years. So I have put the chapters together so they constitute a single cruise from north to south but I have left in the dates of the original trips.

I have indicated where I used quotes from articles in the New York Times for chapters 12 and 14 about Fire Island and Staten Island respectively and the Wall Street Journal for chapter 19 about Dufuskie Island South Carolina.

Finally an apology. It is difficult to write about coastal policy without referring to Presidential policies about things like climate change, FEMA and federal flood insurance. So I apologize in advance for the many times President Trump intruded on this story but it seems like that was just the way it was during this last turbulent year.

Ipswich, 2017

Acknowledgements

I have mentioned most of the people who helped me gather material for this book in the text. However I would like to especially thank several people who went way beyond the call of duty.

They include Becky Coburn who designed the cover and stewarded the manuscript through the entire publication process.

They include my friend and inestimable editor Richard Lodge at the Newburyport Daily where many of these chapters were first published. A few of the chapters have also appeared in earlier books.

They include the excellent photographers, Ethan Cohen and Sandy Tilton. Sandy uses her keen eye to observe the beauty of coastal processes while Ethan uses his drone to give us the big picture. Andy Griffith and Plum Island Outdoors have given us the opportunity to do much of this photography.

I would also like to thank the good people at the Quebec Labrador Foundation, The Sounds Conservancy, and the Institution for Savings, and Storm Surge for providing grants to help fund the research for this book.

And most of all I'd like to thank Kristina and Chappell for putting up with my spending long stormy nights up to my keister in cold water and long steamy days sitting on my keister typing notes in our attic.

Introduction
One Lousy Birthday Present
June 1, 2017

Mar-a-Lago

I was born on June 1 1946. On June 1 2017, Donald Trump removed the Unites States from the Paris Climate Accords. During those intervening 70 odd years I had watched the United States become the largest emitter of green house gases in the world. I had watched us go from being one-car families with radios, to SUV owners with flat screens, computers, and mobile phones.

I had watched us go from taking car trip vacations to thinking nothing about flying all over the world for business and recreation. I had watched us go from eating meat and potatoes from nearby farms to having exotic food flown in from all over the globe. I had watched our rivers, streams, and air become polluted and houses wash into the ocean because of climate change and sea level rise.

But I had also seen the United States become the dominant world power maintaining the peace and offering hope, aid and a symbol of freedom and democracy to the rest of the world.

During my student years I studied biology, geology and international law to help me be able to do something about these problems. In recent years I helped start a local environmental group and wrote four books about erosion on Plum Island in northern Massachusetts. It had taken 5 years, but I think Plum Islanders have started to learn how to work with nature to slow erosion and protect their homes.

We had helped disseminate the first piece of solid science to come out about Plum Island erosion in over forty years. We had been instrumental in convincing the Commonwealth of Massachusetts to build a $150,000 dual dune system to protect homes with local sources of sand. We had helped convince the city of Newburyport to provide $8,000 along with the 15 other communities on the Merrimack River to keep floating debris, including heroin needles, from flushing down the river and ending up in parks and on public beaches.

But that had all changed with a single stroke of a pen. President Trump had "made America great again", right down there with Syria and Nicaragua, the only other countries who had refused to sign the Paris Climate Accords — Nicaragua because it didn't feel the Accords went far enough, and more recently Turkey because it would not get paid by the United States to reduce its carbon footprint.

To make matters worse I even lost 50 cents on a long shot bet I had made that Secretary of State Rex Tillerson would somehow convince Trump to stay in the Accords. As a New Englander I wasn't quite sure what bothered me more, the end of the world or losing my 50 cents.

INTRODUCTION
JUNE 1, 2017

But I resolved then and there, on my 71st birthday, to take the battle to Donald Trump sitting in his palatial Mar-a-Lago estate only four feet above the sea. This is the story of my journey to explore the effects of our exiting the Paris Climate Accords on coastal communities from Plum Island to Palm Beach.

Chapter 1
The 2017 Hurricane Season
June 1, 2017

Hurricane Season

The same day Donald Trump withdrew from the Paris Climate Accords was also the official start of the 2017 hurricane season. The National Weather Service had forecast that it would be a particularly active season with 5 to 9 hurricanes, 11 to 17 named storms, and 2 to 4 major hurricanes. Satellite imagery had shown that El Niño had ceased in the Pacific Ocean and the Atlantic Ocean would be hotter than usual, creating ideal conditions for major hurricanes.

But there was another reason the 2017 hurricane season would be so dangerous. In addition to pulling out of the Climate Accords, Trump's administration planned to cut funding for the system of satellites that provided data for forecasting things like hurricanes, El Niños and climate change events.

This meant that living on the coast would return to what it had been before hurricane forecasting, when 6,000 people were swept into the Gulf of Mexico because they had no warning of the 1900 Galveston Storm, or when 600 people were swept off a Long Island beach during the 1938 Hurricane. They had flocked to the beach to see a mysterious fog bank that turned out to be the storm surge of the swiftly approaching storm. Nobody knew the storm was coming because the U. S. still didn't have a system for forecasting hurricanes.

The first hurricane warning service had been started in the 1870's in Cuba. Father Benito Venes had noticed that clouds preceded hurricanes as the storms passed from one side of Cuba to the other. He was able to use those observations to predict hurricanes days in advance. One reason that the Galveston storm had been so devastating is that the U.S. weather service had refused to incorporate Benito's observations into their daily weather reports.

But by the 1950's the US weather service was using aircraft to forecast hurricanes and they had started to name the storms after their pilot's girlfriends. They could forecast a storm a day in advance in 1954, two days in advance by 1961, 3 days by 1964 and 5 days by 2001. If we

Chapter 1
The 2017 Hurricane Season

want to achieve similar advances, we have to continue improving our satellite system to provide data for more accurate models.

When coastal communities are destroyed by hurricanes today, it is usually not so much a natural catastrophe as a man-made disaster brought about by people building homes on treacherous coastal cliffs and vulnerable barrier beaches.

I had been writing about one of these barrier beaches, Plum Island, since Hurricane Sandy. Because 2017 was also going to be the fifth anniversary of that storm, I decided to start my trip by looking at Plum Island on the Northern coast of Massachusetts, where a lot was still going on.

Chapter 2
The Boat Wreck
Plum Island, Massachusetts
June 6, 2017

Coast Guard Cutter in the mouth of the Merrimack River

"Now why would anyone want to go out in a boat on such a cold, windy day?" wondered Roxanne Lewis as she watched two men launch their small craft from Cashman's Landing.

Forty-five minutes later the men were wallowing in the 8-foot waves and swift currents in the mouth of what the U.S. Coast guard calls the most dangerous river entrance on the East Coast. One of the waves smashed their boat into the Merrimack River's North Jetty flipping it over and throwing both men into the forty-degree water.

At 6pm the Coast Guard's 47-foot life saving boat arrived and her crewmen were able to throw a buoy to one of the men but he was so exhausted he couldn't hold on. The second man was just able to crawl onto the slippery boulders of the jetty where a fireman from Salisbury found him. The man was cold, wet and inconsolable from seeing his friend drift slowly away before going under.

It was a reminder that even though the worst of the erosion season was over, the mouth of the Merrimack River was still the most dangerous place to operate a boat on the East Coast, and Plum Island was among the most dangerous places to own a coastal home.

Chapter 3
Plum Island

Bennett Hill, Plum Island

I didn't have far to go far to discover how New England was faring five years after Hurricane Sandy. Our own backyard had suffered as much as almost any other spot. I drove to Plum Island to take a look. For the past 40 years Plum Island had been New England's poster child for everything you shouldn't do to a barrier beach.

Groins built in the Sixties created a hotspot of erosion that led to 8 houses being lost and 39 being condemned in 2013. A half-mile long illegal seawall failed and was rebuilt in 2013, 2014 and 2015. A jetty, repaired in 2014, put 250 more houses at risk on the northern tip of the island.

All these projects had been undertaken without doing studies into the actual coastal geology of the area. The resulting damage had been caused more by the hand of man than the hand of nature.

I had spent the night before Sandy filming as Plum Island residents used an oversized bulldozer to scrape sand off the public beach at low tide and pile it up into a 40-foot high artificial sand dune against their homes' foundations. The storm surge had swept the sand dune away in the next tidal cycle, leaving staircases dangling in the air 40 feet above the empty beach.

Even so, New England had dodged a bullet. If the storm had arrived ten hours earlier or ten hours later, New England would have suffered the same amount of damage as New York or New Jersey. But Sandy had arrived at low tide so its storm surge and waves were a good 12 feet lower than if the storm had arrived just a few hours before or after.

But, if the damage that happened on the north end of Plum Island was caused by human activities, I wanted to find out what had happened to the southern end of the island where there were no anti-erosion structures.

I could have driven half an hour north to Newbury, then half an hour south on Plum Island. Instead I launched my kayak from Pavilion Beach and made the trip in 15 minutes.

My water route was so short because the southern end of Plum Island starts in Ipswich, then stretches north 8 miles to protect the towns of Rowley, Newbury and Newburyport. I can't vouch for the good people of Rowley and the Newburys but I know Ipswichites are concerned about what will happen when the Atlantic Ocean bursts through Plum Island's barrier beach.

But the water crossing was not without its own perils. I had to make my way a hundred yards upstream, then paddle furiously straight across the current making sure I didn't get swamped in someone's wake or get swept into the open Atlantic by the outgoing tide.

Chapter 3
Plum Island

But the short trip to the Sandy Point State Park was well worth it. I found myself on one of the most beautiful beaches on the East Coast. Every year the end of the point grows as sand is eroded out the center of the island to build up a half a mile wide shelf of sparkling white sand and turquoise water. It made me feel like I was bone fishing on the Bahaman Banks.

Endangered piping plovers dashed comically in and out of receding waves and flocks of terns jostled for airspace over schools of silversides driven to the surface by striped bass. The bass had arrived the night before to feed on millions of squid that had congregated just offshore to lay their masses of gelatinous eggs.

Now many of the long stringy masses of eggs torn off the bottom by last night's storm glistened in the late afternoon sun. The eggs would probably die, but it seemed of little consequence in the face of such rampant fecundity.

What I didn't see was any kind of human tragedy. Just plants, fish, birds and people taking advantage of the beach adapting naturally to sea level rise. It brought home the point that a beach without human structures never suffers from erosion. It just grows, pulsates and changes after every storm as nature intended it to.

Chapter 4
At A Horseshoe Crab Orgy
Pleasant Bay
June 9, 2017

Mating horseshoe crabs

The moon is full. There is no wind. There are no sounds save for the quiet lapping of the water against the shore. It is the Ninth of June. The beach quietly awaits the flood tide, the highest of the month. An expectant sense of creation fills the heavy night air, for it was in warm shallow waters like these where life first evolved.

Offshore, a female horseshoe crab is preparing to reenact a ritual that has persisted for over 400 Million year. Heavy with the weight of thousands of tiny green eggs she advances slowly toward the shore. She must crawl through a stag line of smaller male horseshoe crabs attracted by pheromones, chemical aphrodisiacs she has released into the still waters.

Gradually the dark forms of the crabs appear in the silvery luminescence of the moon as they start their long crawl up the beach. The quiet scraping and scratching of their shells can be heard as they clamber over each other in their eagerness to lay and fertilize her eggs, for soon the tide will turn, stranding them in the heat of the early morning sun.

But there is something wrong on this beach. For a hundred meters to the left and right, the shore is littered with the shells of large dead female horseshoe crabs. It is the same with all the beaches on this bay. If you add them all up it would come to about 30,000 dead crabs or about a third of all the mature crabs in Pleasant Bay.

This is not a natural phenomenon. If you look carefully you can see a small puncture wound in the leathery hinge in the middle of each crab's back. A small blob of blue blood laced with fungal infection oozes from the wounds of some of the more freshly bled crabs.

Anything that comes in contact with the human blood system, whether it be a vaccine, syringe, scalpel or artificial knee joint has to be tested to make sure it is free of Gram negative bacteria, that are as deadly as they are ubiquitous in warm shallow waters like these. The way these medical products are tested is with a reagent distilled from the copper based blood of the horseshoe crab called Limulus amoebocyte lysate, or LAL for short. The bottom line of all this is that processed horseshoe crab is worth over $15,000 a quart.

It is safe to say that every man, woman and child in the United States has been protected by this wild animal that is declining up and down the East Coast. And now large new markets for LAL are opening up in China and India, which will put more pressure on our East Coast crabs.

The story of horseshoe crabs changes about every decade. When I first started writing about them in the early Seventies, a scientist at the Woods Hole Oceanographic Institution was bleeding about a hundred

Chapter 4
At A Horseshoe Crab Orgy Pleasant Bay

crabs a week in his basement and had just filed papers with the FDA to sell LAL to his fellow researchers for about $250 a pop.

He filed under Associates of Cape Cod, the name of his wife's small real estate firm. In those innocent early days the company bled less than a thousand crabs a summer. All of them were returned to Pleasant Bay and mortality from bleeding and transporting the crabs was less than 10%, though the company boasted that no crabs died during the process.

Now the former mom and pop firm is owned by the Tokyo based multi-national Seikegaku, which had bought the firm for over $30 Million dollars. They bleed about 200,000 crabs a summer delivered to them from as far away as Virginia and mortality from their bleeding, transporting and handling the crabs is over 30%.

But today scientists are studying exactly what kills the crabs during transportation, bleeding and handling to see how practices could be changed to save the animals that have protected so many human lives. Some of the best research is taking place at the Jackson Estuarine Lab on Great Bay in nearby New Hampshire. I decided to drive up there to see some of their research and compare Pleasant Bay with a virgin area where horseshoe crabs had never been collected for biomedical purposes.

Chapter 5
The Jackson Lab
Durham, NH
June 27, 2017

Searching for horseshoe crabs in Durham New Hampshire

I have always been fascinated with marine research stations, whether they be the Marine Biological Lab in Woods Hole, the Bermuda Biological Station in St Georges, or La Parguera Station in Puerto Rico. The idea of having a group of intelligent people working together to understand the intricacies of nature in an isolated, often exotic environment is compelling — if not a little romantic.

The Jackson Estuarine Laboratory in Durham, New Hampshire is no exception. Sun dappled woods and broad green fields roll down to the rocky shores of Great Bay.

I arrived on June 27, just in time to join Win Watson, Chris Chabot and Meghan Owings as they dodged rainsqualls to survey the shore. The first thing I noticed was that there were no dead horseshoe crabs. On Pleasant Bay we would have encountered at least 50 dead crabs on such a 100-meter transect.

The second thing I noticed was how neat everything was. If this were a collecting area, you would see boats, car buoys, offshore pens, pens in marshes, even old boats on the shore to hold crabs overnight before they could be trucked to one of the bleeding facilities. Plus, you would see several people loading plastic trash cans full of horseshoe crabs into trucks or onto boats to be returned to the water.

Here you only had the three scientists lavishing care on about 65 crabs. But what they were doing was replicating a commercial bleeding operation, to get a detailed picture of morbidity from the entire process.

They had captured the crabs and left them in the sun on the roof of their lab for several hours to simulate conditions aboard a collecting boat. Then they had actually put them in trashcans and driven them around for 4 hours to simulate transportation to the bleeding facility.

Then they had bled a third of each crabs' blood and kept them overnight in a tank before attaching pingers to the crabs and releasing them back into Great Bay. There they could use signals from the pingers to monitor how far the crabs moved and if the crabs could still discern tidal patterns so they could lay their eggs on the furthest incursions of the next full moon high tide.

What they found is that not only had the combination of desiccation, transportation, bleeding and handling led to 30% of the crabs dying, but that a ganglion just below the hinge where they had been bled had been damaged, so the crabs had also lost the ability to keep track of tidal cycles. Plus, removing hemocyanin and amoebocyte cells from their blood had compromised the crabs' immune systems. So even if

Chapter 5
The Jackson Lab Durham, NH

they had survived the multiple traumas associated with handling and bleeding, it was unlikely the crabs would be able to reproduce that summer, and in future years they might even produce fewer eggs.

This accounted for the anomaly in the records of the Northeast states that showed that despite regulations that restricted the capture of crabs, their populations were still declining.

The team made the point that they didn't want to shut down the bleeding operations, but their data made the point that since almost two thirds of the mortality came from transportation and handling of the crabs, it made sense to cut down on that first, then improve how the crabs were bled later.

A few of the lysate companies avoided such collateral damage by having their bleeding facilities situated on the water so the crabs could be bled and returned to the wild within a few hours. This also reduced the amount of contamination that occurred when you had the bleeding area and the production area under the same roof.

Cross-contamination had become such a problem in some of the companies that the FDA had shut them down temporarily and recommended that they separate their bleeding and production facilities. The FDA could require that all the companies start doing the same thing.

This would allow the raw lysate facilities to concentrate on improving their bleeding operations by following some of the Jackson Lab's recommendations. One would be to stop inserting their needles directly into the crab's hinge and start inserting them from an angle to avoid damaging the tidal sensing ganglion. Another would be to suffuse the crabs' holding tanks with copper supplements to increase their production of hemocyanin before they were released back into the natural environment.

If all these practices became standard procedure the crabs should continue to be keystone species for East Coast's many estuaries, continue to provide millions of tons of eggs to several species of endangered migrating birds and continue to protect the lives of every man, woman and child in the United States — and soon the world.

Not a bad trick for a single species of wild animal that has been crawling through our planet's estuaries since way before there were birds, fish, mammals, even humans to greet and bleed them.

Chapter 6
The Devil Wears Pinstripes
Plum Island
June 19, 2017

Illegal seawall.

On June 19, President Trump borrowed a page from George W. Bush's playbook by nominating ten Federal Court justices at the same time. It was the opening salvo in what could become a four-year war to pack the federal courts with handpicked conservative judges.

For coastal dwellers, one nominee stood out in particular. Damian Schiff was the senior staff attorney for the Pacific Legal Foundation, the oldest and most powerful anti-environmental organization in the country.

"The Foundation" cut its teeth arguing that cigarettes didn't cause lung cancer at the behest of the Phillips Tobacco Company, and then had gone on to litigating for the oil, nuclear, and mining industries with funding from folks like the Koch Brothers.

In recent years The Foundation has helped eviscerate the Environmental Protection Agency, the Endangered Species Act, the Clean Water Act and litigated against local coastal regulations. Damien Schiff had even taken the time to blog that Supreme Court Justice Anthony Kennedy was a "judicial prostitute" and that the California Anti-Bullying program was wrong to propose a lesson plan teaching that kids from homosexual families should have the same rights as kids from heterosexual ones.

Massachusetts's officials had first encountered The Foundation's strong-arm tactics when the state tried to uphold its own environmental restrictions against building seawalls on Plum Island. One of the homeowners was on the board of directors of the Foundation and had their lawyers call then Governor Duvall Patrick, threatening to sue the state.

Half an hour after the call, the state backed down, leaving an illegal seawall that made the public beach inaccessible and swimming treacherous, At the same time the costly seawall had done nothing to stop erosion to the houses that had been permitted to be rebuilt on exactly the same footprint as before they had washed away during the March storm in 2013. Would I find similar examples of the Pacific Legal Foundation using their deep pockets and legal muscle to block local regulations as I traveled to Mar-a-Lago? I would soon find out.

Chapter 7
Donald and The Iceberg
July 12, 2017

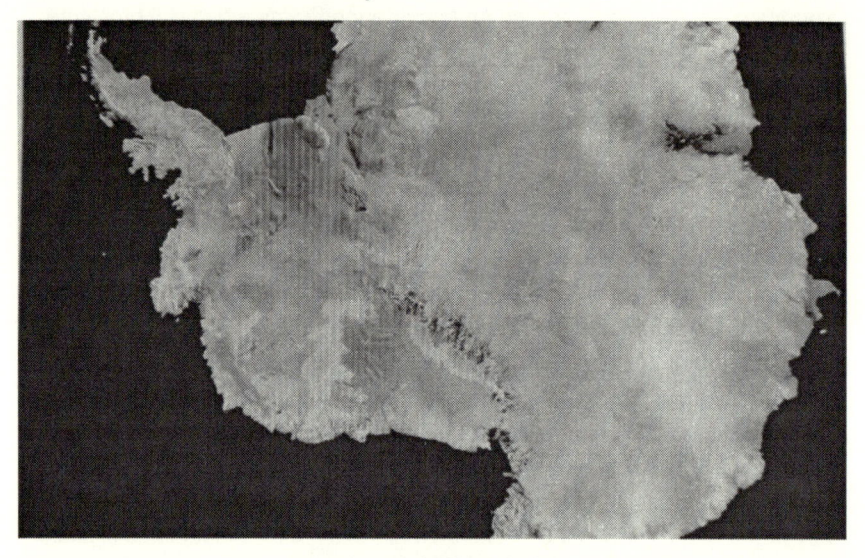

Larsen ice shelf on the left

On July 12, 2017 a trillion ton iceberg the size of Delaware calved off from the Antarctica peninsula. It floated almost as high above water as the Eiffel Tower and three times deeper underwater. On the same day it was revealed that Donald Trump Jr. had e-mailed, "I love it!" in response to a Russian lawyer's invitation to share dirt on Hilary Clinton. Now I'm sure "I love it!" will go right down there with "I'm not a crook," and "It depends what your definition of is, is," as iconic defenses of presidential cover-ups.

If we were on a planet governed by Vulcans, or if "no drama Obama" were still in office, the mainstream media would be so afraid that he might start repeating his three main points about the Affordable Health Care Act that they would have run the Iceberg story front page, above the fold. And the Vulcan president would have proposed funding research on the problem and contacted all the other Vulcan nations about curtailing emissions for the long-term future of their planet.

Unfortunately, rather than being on a rerun of *Star Trek* we seem to stuck in *Dumb and Dumber.* And our instinct driven leaders seem more intent on short-term gain than long term survival.

So, instead of working to solve this difficult problem, we do what any social primate would do, concentrate on the foibles and sex lives of our leaders. We seem far more interested in why Melania wont hold Donald Trump's hand than that pesky little iceberg floating somewhere off Antarctica.

The Trump Jr. saga will dominate the news cycles for several months, but which incident will have greater significance twenty or even fifty years from now, another scandal in this scandal ridden presidency or enough sea level rise to start threatening Boston, London, Shanghai and Miami?

That is the concern of scientists who have been monitoring the break up of Antarctica's Ice Shelf that acts like a cork holding back the Antarctica's land-based glaciers. The last time the planet was warming this fast was 125,000 years ago and the sea levels rose 25 to 30 feet higher than today. What they don't know is how quickly that happened, was it over centuries or thousands of years, or over just decades like what we have just seen on the ice shelf of the Antarctic Peninsula?

Probably the most authoritative analysis of this problem was done by James Hansen and 18 other scientists. They calculated that due to all causes we can expect nine feet of sea level rise in 50 years and about three feet in 25 years. An earlier paper figured out that when the seas start rising more than 3 feet a century, barrier beaches like Plum Island will start breaking up rather than migrating slowly landward.

Chapter 7
Donald and The Iceberg

Ever since the Ice Age the sea has been rising about a foot every century, but about twenty years ago that rose to about a foot and a half feet. So people have had the experience of going to a beach that they remembered as a kid being sixty to a hundred feet wide and now seeing waves lapping at the dunes.

Nauset, the beach I went to as a child has retreated so far that the town of Orleans has bought a nearby motel's empty parking lot so they can start using it when their old lot is washed away. Just this past summer they moved several of their buildings dozens of feet further back.

If the Hansen paper is correct our kids will see the retreats of whole sections of cities like Newburyport and the disappearance of beautiful barrier islands like Plum Beach in the face of this onslaught.

Chapter 8
Dual Wing Bars
Plum Island Point
July 16, 2017

Wing Bar Fishing on Plum Island Point

I was finally able to make it out to Plum Island Point on July 16. I hadn't been out here for over a month because of a long story. A wild skunk had attacked and scratched my wife, and I got pneumonia from sitting in the Emergency Room waiting for my initial 7 shots.

So I was delighted to see several people fishing along the edge of two sandbars. But two of the fishermen were a hundred feet offshore and up to their armpits in water.

This was a great place to fish. Striped bass lurked in the deep holes beside the bars waiting to ambush baitfish that were being swept overhead. They were easy prey. The change from salt water to fresh had disoriented them, making them easy to catch. Terns had also assembled, raucously plunging into the water to snap up the disabled baitfish.

But it not such a good place to stand. At any moment the fishermen could step in a hole, the tide could change, or an errant wave could knock them off their feet and they could swept up in the outgoing current and be way over their heads in boat traffic. The year before, a fourteen year old girl had to be rescued after being swept off this same sandbar and the year before that a great white shark had attacked a seal along this same shore.

I was surprised to see that the wing bar we had been watching for two years had grown north and a second wing bar had formed to the south. Wing bars are constantly moving objects that form where the outflowing current of a river meets the flow of the incoming high tides. They are usually adjacent to the flood tide delta, a delta of sand pushed into the mouth of the river by the incoming tides.

This past spring the flow of the river was strong and the tides were moderate, so the tidal and riverine currents had colluded to push the wing bar south. But now that it was the summer, the tides were strong and the river flow was low, so the currents had shifted the wing bar north almost a hundred feet.

That accounted for the northern wing bar, but what about the southern one? The southern one occurred at low tide when the outflow of the river was strong enough to overpower the tidal currents. Then the river current clashed with longshore currents pushing sand along this shore from where it had washed through the jetty. Together the two currents clashing from north and south had created this hundred-foot sandbar jutting out perpendicularly from the shore.

This was a pretty auspicious development, not only for fishermen, but for the homeowners on Northern Reservation Terrace as well. It meant that more sand was in the sand transport system in front of their homes. It also meant that sand eroding off the end of North Point was silting under the docks of the Captain's Lady's fishing boats.

Chapter 8
Dual Wing Bars Plum Island Point

The owner of the charter boats, George Charos, had already applied for permits to dredge the sand and give it to the state so the state could rebuild the dunes in front of the houses on Northern Reservation Terrace. All that was needed was money and permits to rebuild the sacrificial dunes that had protected the houses so well the year before. Hopefully that would be arranged at the next meeting of the Merrimack River Beach User's Alliance.

If everything fell into place at exactly the right time the sacrificial dunes would give nature enough time to lower the jetty so enough sand could flow through so the beach could start growing again.

Chapter 9
Reflections on Erosion
Thacher Island
July 2017

Thacher island

By mid-summer I decided it was time to reestablish my sea legs by visiting nearby Thacher island, where 22 colonists died in what was probably the most severe hurricane to ever strike New England, the Great Colonial Hurricane of 1635.

In 1635, the minister from my own hometown, Ipswich, was taking his wife, son and cousins to Marblehead where he was going to take over as pastor of the Methodist Church. But just as their small bark rounded Cape Ann it was beset with ferocious winds. Of course they had had no warning because there were no weather forecasts to go on. And even though the hurricane had brushed past the Jamestown Colony, knocked down thousands of trees and killed 11 Native Americans outside the Plymouth Plantation, they had no way of knowing it happened only hours before.

The winds smashed the boat onto Rockport's Crackwoods Ledge throwing Reverend Avery, his wife and eldest son into the sea along with all their cousins. Mr. Thacher and his daughter were thrown up onto the rocky shore of what would become known as Thacher's island. The next wave washed Reverend Avery and his son back into the maelstrom and they would never be seen again. But Mrs. Thacher had been lashed to the bowsprit and she and her husband were the only survivors of the wreck that had taken the lives of 22 people.

The storm had probably caused the highest storm surge to ever engulf the New England coast. You can still see where it left a steeply eroded scarp all along the western edge of the Gulf of Maine.

Fortunately the weather was far better when we cruised out on a landing craft owned by the Thacher Island Association. I learned that the island's first lighthouse had been built in 1771. But townspeople thought it was aiding the British finding the approach to Boston more than it helped local captains, so the Gloucester militia sailed to the island and burned the lighthouse down. They also brought the lighthouse keeper back to

Chapter 9
Reflections on Erosion Thacher Island

the mainland. It was never clear whether the militia suspected the light keeper had been purposefully aiding the enemy or not.

But the most notorious resident of the island was Joe "The Animal" Barbosa who the FBI placed on Thacher Island as part of their witness protection program. Joe had been a hit man for Boston's famed Raymond Patriarca crime family. He had earned his sobriquet in a Revere bar where he punched a man in the face and was told by his boss Joe Tameleo to keep his effin' hands to himself for the rest of the night.

Brooding, Joe returned to the bar, then suddenly leaned over and bit the ear off his assailant, snarling to his boss, "Hey, I didn't touch him wid my hands." It was stated by witnesses that he also chewed off his assailant's cheek. But hey, that was never proven.

Joe became embroiled in the gang warfare between the Patriaca Family and Whitey Bulger's Winter Hill gang, reportedly killing as many as 20 people before becoming an informant, allegedly saying something like, "The Patriarch family screwed me so now I'm going to screw as many of them as possible."

Joe ended up at Fulsome Prison where he wrote several books and poems about Boston's gangland warfare before he was gunned down getting into his "James Bond car," a 1965 Oldsmobile Cutlass specially modified to shoot black smoke out the tailpipe at the push of a button. A multitalented man, he also graduated from culinary school and was said to be a talented chef. So I'm sure everyone ate very well during his short stay on Thacher Island.

Fortunately, none of my fellow passengers looked like they were also in the witness protection program and our trip went smoothly.

Chapter 10
"The Long Island Express"
September 15, 1938

1938 Hurricane, courtesy Google Images

In June I was asked to give a talk in Woods Hole Massachusetts so I decided to use the trip to investigate what had happened to the area during the 1938 Hurricane, the most deadly storm to ever strike New England.

A Brazilian freighter first reported the storm off Florida on September 15 1938. It was a late season Cape Verdean hurricane that had developed unnoticed off the coast of Africa and then been nourished by the unusually warm waters of the Atlantic.

By the time the U.S. Weather Bureau heard about it, all they could do was issue a hurried warning for Miami. But during the night the hurricane had unexpectedly veered north, missing the Southeast mainland altogether.

It was swerving around a Bermuda High so the weather Service figured it would continue to blow safely out to sea. But the Bermuda high had itself moved north, nudging the storm over the steamy waters of the Gulf Stream. There, it sucked up more energy and picked up speed, becoming what became known as "The Long Island Express", the fastest moving hurricane in history.

By the afternoon of September 21, the sky had grown dark and telephone poles were snapping like matchsticks all along Long Island, but people continued to stand on the beach mesmerized by a low-lying fogbank hanging just offshore. Of course it wasn't a fogbank, it was the gray waters of the storm's 30-foot high storm surge that swept hundreds of people to their deaths as the winds rose to over 120 miles per hour, on the top of the Empire State Building.

Bob Thielen, a writer for the New Yorker, was vacationing in his summer camp on Martha's Vineyard with his wife Virginia and their maid Lucy from Jamaica. By lunchtime the sky turned an ominous yellow and as Lucy laid out the plates she kept muttering, "This is hurricane weather. We've got to get out of here."

"Nonsense Lucy," Virginia reassured her. "We never get hurricanes this far north."

But, of course this was the hurricane of 1938 and an hour later the wind was making a continuous booming sound that Virginia remembered sounding like, "giant kettle drums beating out wild crescendos." Fearing that the camp would be swept into the sea, the three quickly donned foul-weather gear and raced outside.

They were running along the beach toward a sand dune on the edge of Stonewall Pond when the spray-flecked waters of the storm surge swirled over the barrier beach lifting the camp off its foundations. Knowing that Lucy couldn't swim, Bob held her hand as they struggled through knee-deep waters against the hundred mile-an-hour winds.

Chapter 10
"The Long Island Express"

Their friend, artist Thomas Hart Benton, was collecting mussels off some rocks as he did every morning for his cash-strapped family. As he and his son T.P. approached Stonewall Pond they saw a twenty foot high wave of blue green water topped with another ten feet of pure white spume come hurtling toward the offshore bar. The wave towered over the tiny running figures for one brief moment before crashing down upon them. For another brief moment they could see the Thielens struggling in neck-deep water, then being swept over their heads into the choppy waters of Stonewall pond.

Bob was still holding Lucy's hand, but his waterlogged pants and boots were pulling them both down, so he took a deep breath and let go of her hand just long enough to dive underwater and strip off the offending clothes. But when he returned to the surface Lucy was nowhere to be found. He dove several more times but to no avail.

Equally worried about Virginia, Bob swam to her side and together they struggled against the strong currents and were able to grab a thorn-covered tangle of wild roses and bayberry bushes and pull themselves exhausted onto the shore. As they lay there panting they looked back through the mist and saw their camp floating lopsided, ready to keel over and sink.

The salt spray stung the couple's eyes as they stumbled through a field and past some cows lying huddled together against the storm. That was when they heard Benton's voice over the wind, "You two – you're damn lucky. Come up to our house, Rita has the fire going. We thought you were gone for sure."

Benton and T.P. helped the shell-shocked couple climb the stairs into their house, where Rita met them with tears streaming down her face. She gave them dry clothes and sat them down in front of the roaring fire. For a while all the two could do was stare silently into the flames while eating Rita's warming casserole.

Bob was still shaking so hard he could barely hold his glass, "Lucy just went down. She just went down. Nowhere to be seen. I should have gone back." Tom and Rita assured him that it would have only been futile and dangerous.

Eventually the hot rum and warm fire did their work and Bob started to relax, "I never did like cows up until today." Tom looked at his friend in utter astonishment.

"Now why in hell do you like cows today?"

"I don't know. It's hard to explain. Seeing them there on the hillside looking so warm and safe," he said quietly before staring back into the fire.

A few days later, Bob wrote about his travails for the New Yorker and Thomas Hart Benton painted, "The Flight of the Thielens," which won him widespread attention.

The masterpiece launched Benton's career as a nationally known artist who traveled, sketchbook in hand, across the country chronicling rural America just as it was disappearing. He went on to illustrate John Steinbeck's classic novel "The Grapes of Wrath," and worked with some of Hollywood's best writers and directors on sets and movie posters. You can still see Benton's work hanging in leading museums and on tour throughout the country.

But you don't see any houses on Stonewall Pond Beach. It has been made into a privately protected wildlife area.

On the mainland, Buzzards Bay, Narragansett Bay and Little Narragansett Bay acted like funnels to squeeze the hurricane's storm surge even higher as it tumbled cars, houses, and debris under 30 feet of muddy water in downtown Providence. The beautiful old Cape Cod cottage that used to house the National Marine Fisheries Laboratory in Woods

Chapter 10
"The Long Island Express"

Hole was washed away and replaced by what could be mistaken for a municipal swimming pool of the Fifties era.

Across the bay, New Bedford was also inundated. It took 30 years but the Army Corps of Engineers was finally brought in to build a multi-million dollar barrier designed to withstand another storm the size the 1938 Hurricane. The gate was closed and protected the city during Hurricane Bob and Hurricane Sandy, but everyone knew they didn't even come close to packing the power of the '38 storm.

But perhaps the most poignant place destroyed by the Hurricane of 1938 was Westerly Rhode Island. There, Fort Road stretched out from Watch Hill to become a several mile long barrier beach with low sand dunes, and magnificent summer homes. The homes, along with their occupants, were swept away without a trace during the horrific storm.

It was noteworthy, however, that local officials decided that it was just too dangerous to rebuild houses on the barrier beach so they turned it into the Napatree Point Wildlife Refuge. You can hike out to the end of the beach today and see an island sitting in the middle of Little Narragansett Bay. It is all that remains of the northern end of the island that was severed off during the storm and migrated to its present location during the intervening years. It is now another public barrier island that helps to protect the mainland.

Not far down the road, the pop star Taylor Swift has upset old timers by building a stone seawall to protect her cliff-side home. They grumble that as a new comer she has not had the time to pick up the wisdom and humility that comes from living on a stormy coast. These two strategies, moving or armoring the coast, continue to be two divergent solutions that communities adopt in the wake of such storms. I expected to see variations on those strategies as we cruised south in the wake of Hurricane Sandy.

46

But what happed to the remnants of the 1938 hurricane? It pushed on up through the Connecticut River Valley leaving a path of destruction from Rhode Island to Montreal. She even toppled the trestle bridge on the top of Mount Washington and left 690 dead bodies in her wake. They died primarily because they had no warning of the storm's approach and didn't know they should evacuate.

Chapter 11
Muskegat Island
1938

"Better get under cover, Sylvester! There's a storm blowing, a whopper! To speak in the vernacular of the peasantry! Poor girl I hope she gets home alright."
- Professor Marvel
<u>The Wizard of Oz</u>
L. Frank Baum, 1900

Muskegat Island, courtesy Crocher Snow family.

Not far away, from the Thielens on Martha's Vineyard, Marcus Dunham was battling for his life on Muskegat, a tiny sand island between Martha's Vineyard and Nantucket. Marcus thought he had been having a dizzy spell when the storm surge floated his camp off its foundation and whirled it around like Dorothy's house in the *Wizard of Oz*.

Marcus had to crawl through a window and dive under the building before it flipped over and sank. But his trek was far from over. He still had to half-wade, half-walk up onto one of the low-lying dunes that were still above water. His rescuers found him in the dune, exhausted but still alive a full day later.

A decade after the storm, Crocker Snow bought Muskegat and its life savings station and started a unique experiment. He kept the island in the family and but let it revert back to nature with Federal recognition as a refuge. Now it is one of the wildest places on the entire East Coast.

From December through March, Muskegat has a post-humankind, post-apocalyptic feel. Its population of gray seals has jumped from 20 individuals in 1985, to over 20,000 in 2015 and the 800-pound behemoths have taken over the island. They slide down its dunes like otters, which is cute but tears up the dune grass. They live on the porch of the Snow's camp, which they defend with slashing incisors. They have picked up avian flu DNA from the island's freshwater ponds, which are filled with seal urine and afterbirth tissue.

You can smell the seals' musky odor a mile off the beach and their incessant bellowing makes it impossible to sleep. It seems like it will only be a matter of time before some young Great White Shark finds this cornucopia of seal flesh and spreads the message by word of mouth.

But so far the water around the island is so shallow that the Great White Sharks avoid it because their favored method of attack is to hide in deep waters and ambush prey swimming overhead. Of course we all know this from reading Jaws, which Peter Benchley wrote in his house on nearby Nantucket.

But the seals seem to think they are safe on the island so they no longer migrate north to Sable Island like the other Gray Seals in Massachusetts. So now close to half of all the Gray Seals in Massachusetts live year-round on Muskegat's 200 acres of relentlessly shifting sand.

Chapter 11
Muskegat Island

But the most fascinating aspect of this island is that the Snow family has willingly retreated from the island and set it up as a place where scientists can come and study the ever-changing ecosystem of birds, fish and seals. It is probably the best example on the East Coast of successfully returning a barrier island back to nature in the face of the sea level rise that will inundate it, probably within fifty years.

Chapter 12
The Silver Lining
Fire Island
2015

Inlet into Pleasant Bay, Cape Cod.

Hurricane Sandy had lifted the Molesphini's house off its pilings and deposited it almost on the other side of Traffic Avenue. Of course the name of the street was ironic. No cars were allowed on this section of Fire Island. You had to take the ferry and walk to your home.

The storm surge had been so gentle that none of the Molesphini's prized wine glasses had been broken in the unplanned move. But the couple had to spend $300,000 to return the house to its original location, raise it on pilings four feet taller than before, and stabilize it with diagonals made from ¾ inch steel rods. However, after almost two years of work, Mr. Molesphini was pleased:

"I would put this house up against another Sandy, any day!"

But the government was another matter. The Army Corps of Engineers decided that the best way to protect Fire Island was to rebuild a sand dune able to run straight and true for 12.5 miles. Unfortunately, Traffic Avenue was right in the way.

Traffic Ave had been built so that it looped out about 30 feet in front of the other streets to give its owners a better view of the Atlantic Ocean. But now, Traffic Avenue had become the weak link in the chain and the Molesphinis and their neighbors had to pay the price. They would have to remove their homes or they would be taken by eminent domain and demolished. The Molesphinis would be paid the full market value of their home but not for the $300,000 they had spent to stormproof it.

Of course you always have winners and losers in real estate. While the homeowners on Traffic Avenue were facing eviction, the value of their neighbors' houses across the street had doubled because they would soon be waterfront homes.

Mr. Molesphinni's neighbor Anthony Lorenzo ruefully explained the situation, "The people behind us had their house on the market for $800,000 after Sandy and they recently said they would sell it to us for $1.4 million because it would soon be waterfront property. They have been our neighbors for 30 years!"

But such gains and losses weren't only restricted to real estate. A little further down the beach, water rushed through an inlet that burst through the barrier beach during Hurricane Sandy. When it first opened, mainland homeowners had lobbied to have the inlet closed to protect their homes on the other side of Great South Bay.

But by the time the Army Corps of Engineers came up with a plan the inlet had stabilized at about 20 feet deep and 1500 feet wide. The day after Hurricane Sandy, it would have taken about thirteen guys with

Chapter 12
The Silver Lining Fire Island

shovels to fill in the inlet. Now it would require expensive dredges and millions of dollars to do the work.

Meanwhile the inlet had built up its own constituency. The first summer after the inlet opened, people started to realize that the bay was as clean as they remembered it as kids. Mike Busch marveled, "Now I can look over the side of my boat and see sea robins lying on the ocean floor eight feet below me."

For the past thirty years huge blooms of brown algae had cut visibility to a scant few feet. The culprit had been the many houses and agricultural fields on Long Island. Tons of pesticides, lawn products and sewage had leached out of leaky septic tanks and washed off lawns and agricultural fields to over-fertilize the waters of Great South Bay. The resultant brown tides had killed off almost all of the shellfish beds that had once supplied half of all the clams consumed in the United States.

Eelgrass is the keystone species of such estuarine environments. It is actually a higher plant, an angiosperm, similar to the flowers you might see in your garden. It has tiny blossoms that bloom in the spring and release their yellowish pollen directly into the salty waters.

Somewhere during its early evolution this former land plant had moved back into shallow saltwater bays where they found no competition and thrived. Because of this strange quirk of evolution, eelgrass has become what scientists call an "indicator species" because it needs clean, clear waters to allow enough sunlight to filter through the water column, so its fronds can photosynthesis. But for the last thirty years the brown tides had blocked out the sun causing most of the eelgrass beds in Great South Bay to blanch and die.

But Hurricane Sandy changed all that. It had burst through the barrier beach delivering millions of gallons of fresh clean salt water. Initially the new inlet was only a few feet deep and about forty feet wide.

In the spring, fishermen had started seeing more fluke, seals and river herring in the bay. They hoped that the new inlet would help resurrect one of the East Coast's only populations of sea run brook trout. Even the clams caught in the Eastern part of the bay had nice big fat growth rings from gorging on all the plankton now rushing through the inlet on every incoming tide.

It would have cost millions of dollars for humans to have made these improvements, but nature had done it for free. However, there was a flip side to this new situation. Politicians had started to pressure the New York Department of Environmental Conservation to close the inlet because many of their constituents lived on the other side of the bay and feared that the break in the barrier beach would leave them susceptible to flooding. They pointed out that the Department had promulgated a breach contingency plan in 1996 that called for closing any inlets that did not fill in naturally.

But the break had already become a popular destination. Boaters now enjoyed swimming and fishing on the shallow flats created by the new inlet and every weekend hundreds of people walked a mile out from Smith Point just to view the new phenomenon.

The Fire Island National Seashore had requested funds to study the inlet, but the Department of Environmental Conservation had already asked the Army Corps of Engineers for a plan to fill the inlet in.

The same thing had happened on Cape Cod. In April 2007, an inlet had broken into Pleasant Bay, but by the time homeowners had a chance to put together a summer town meeting, the price tag to fill in the inlet had risen to $4.1 Million dollars. And on foggy nights the signs that homeowners had posted to read "Save our Shores" would somehow be altered to read "Save our Inlet".

Chapter 12
The Silver Lining Fire Island

So, on a sweltering night in late July, when the town moderator finally intoned, "All those in favor of the town's borrowing $4.1 Million dollars to fill in the inlet say aye" only two defiant voices answered in the positive.

"Those opposed?"

Six hundred "No's" roared back like a wave of rolling thunder.

Now I know New Yorkers are known more for their chutzpah than their wisdom. But one might hope that in this one small instance they will follow the lead of their neighbors to the north. Of course they never have before, so why should I expect them to this time?

Chapter 13
Hurricane Sandy
Oceanside, Long Island
October 29, 2012

The day after Hurricane Sandy

The south side of Long Island is where late season Cape Verdean hurricanes usually hit the United States first. This was where the several hundred people had been swept off the beach during the 1938 hurricane.

But Robin and Dennis Covelli weren't that concerned. Weather forecasting had greatly improved. Plus, they had already survived several hurricanes, both on Long Island where they lived, and in North Carolina where they planned to retire.

Their house was in Oceanside, set back from Great South Bay which was itself protected by Long Beach over 5 miles away. Dennis figured they could ride out Sandy as they had all the other hurricanes.

But when he went out the morning before Sandy arrived, Dennis saw something he had never seen before. Water had risen so high in the canal 500 feet from his house, that it had flooded the streets. He couldn't even wade to the corner.

So this was the storm surge the weather forecasters kept talking about. If this was what it was like at low tide what would it be like when the water would be nine feet higher at high tide? It didn't matter that the ocean was 5 miles away. He had forgotten about that damn canal.

Dennis rushed back to the house; they packed the family into the car and drove to Robin's mother's house in Queens. It was fortunate they left. That night several of their neighbors who lived in basement apartments died when the water rose up to the ceiling. Struggle as they might, they couldn't find any pockets of air to keep from drowning.

Two days after the storm Dennis drove back to Oceanside. But before he was even five miles from his house he knew something was wrong. Flooded cars and fallen trees were strewn across the streets, and it took him two more hours to finally reach their home.

But he couldn't believe it when he opened the front door. The stench was overwhelming. Their basement was still full of water and there were ugly brown watermarks, four feet high up on the walls of their kitchen and living room. All their clothes, furniture and household items were completely destroyed.

Every time Dennis opened another kitchen cabinet water would pour out along with soggy lumps of congealed sugar, pasta and cereal. The refrigerator reeked of rotting meat and decaying vegetables.

Chapter 13
Hurricane Sandy Oceanside, Long Island

Their neighbors had already started to haul clothes, furniture and mattresses into the street where they would sit in giant moldy piles that the rats would find before they could be disposed of by the disabled trash department garbage trucks.

Dennis was still in shock when he heard a knock on the door. It was the contractor who had remodeled their house only a few months before. Dennis started to say he was in no condition to make any decisions. But Tom cut him off.

"Don't worry about it, Dennis. I'll take care of everything."

It was the best thing that could have ever happened. Tom Cabretta had worked on several other houses in the neighborhood so their owners had readily agreed to his suggestion that he repair all of their houses at the same time.

By doing so, he was able to save time by using the Covelli's garage as a staging area to cache lumber and another neighbor's garage to cache sheetrock and whitewall materials. This allowed him to buy in bulk while building supplies were still available, and then concentrate on finishing the job.

The Covellis stayed at Robin's mother's house for two weeks and then switched over to Dennis' mother's house for several more months while the work was being done. Even so, Jonathan and Michelle had to miss months of school along with tens of thousands of other students.

But the Covellis were lucky. They had some money set aside so they could give Tom the go ahead to start work before their insurance company paid them for their losses.

As it was, the company only paid them $50,000 even though they had sustained $80,000 in damages. But FEMA was the real joke. Dennis stood in line for hours to apply for a living stipend but as soon as the officials heard he had his own insurance company, they dropped him like a hot potato.

The Covellis had lost two of their three cars, their house, and almost everything they owned. But at least they had already decided to retire to North Carolina , so they had a plan. This allowed them to fix up their house and put it on the market before there were too many other houses for sale in the ravaged neighborhood.

It only took the Covellis 5 months to find a buyer and they probably sold the house for $200,000 less than they would have been able to sell it for before the storm. But the price was enough to allow them to buy a new house in North Carolina.

But they had learned their lesson. The Covelli's new house was also 5 miles from the ocean, whereas in Oceanside they had only been nine feet above sea level. Ocean Isle was 56 feet above sea level.

Robin summed up the situation perfectly, "We are extremely fortunate. Every morning we feel like we have died and gone to heaven."

But Dennis has a variation on the theme; "You know that old adage, that anything that doesn't kill you makes you stronger? Well I don't believe it any more!"

Chapter 14
Staten Island

"Let's recognize that there are some places that Mother Nature owns. She may only come to visit every two, or three or every four years. But when she comes to visit, she reclaims the site. I want to be there for people and communities who want to say, I'm going to give this parcel back to Mother Nature."
- Governor Cuomo
February 26, 2013

The Verrazano Bridge, Staten Island on right, Brooklyn on left

OK, I'll admit it. As a New Englander I've never really understood how all of New York's confusing boroughs and islands actually fit together. But when you are on a boat it all starts to make sense. Staten Island and Brooklyn are large masses of land that protect Manhattan from the south.

That is also the reason that Staten Island and the Brooklyn end of Long Island accounted for most of New York City's 43 fatalities during Sandy. The hurricane's storm surge was funneled into Staten Island, where it racked the south shore from the Verrazano Narrows to Tottenville.

You can also see how selective Sandy was when she devastated this coast. Oakwood Heights looks like nothing ever happened, just a bunch of middle class homes clustered around the railway station where the real estate market is booming.

But when you step across Hylan Boulevard, you enter a different world. Oakwood Beach used to be a thriving working class community. It was the kind of neighborhood where everyone looked after their neighbor's homes and children played in the streets.

But since Hurricane Sandy, everyone has gone. A lone tire swing hangs from an old oak tree. It is the only reminder that children once played in this neighborhood of idyllic little bungalows.

Unfortunately, Oakwood Beach is now remembered more for its three residents who died in their homes during Hurricane Sandy. Two of them had been Neil Filipowicz's brother and nephew. They both drowned in the twenty-foot waves and eight-foot storm surge that inundated their single family home. The third had been Patty Snyder's brother who had stayed behind to protect their home after the rest of the extended family had left for higher ground.

But Oakwood Beach had always been a world apart, a low-lying area of marshes and scrub oak beside the raging Atlantic. Its tallest feature was a mountain of household trash in the center of what had once been

Chapter 14
Staten Island

the largest man-made object on the face of the Globe, the nearby Fresh Kills Landfill.

Every day barges would dump 650 more tons of trash from Manhattan and New Jersey onto the artificial landform. Every day the mountain would grow a little taller. By 2001 it was 25 meters, taller than the Statue of liberty and well on it's way to becoming the highest point on the East Coast.

Then on March 22, 2001 the landfill was closed under pressure from neighbors who feared its packs of roaming feral dogs and hated its reputation as a dumping ground for crooks who got whacked by the mafia. But it was reopened after 9/11 only a few months later. Fresh Kills was the only landfill on the East Coast large enough to accommodate all the rubble and bits and pieces of human remains from the World Trade Center.

But by 2012 most of the former landfill had been reclaimed into the marshes, swamps and oak forests of the Gateway National Park, and New York City's largest recreational area, weighing in at three times larger than New York's Central Park.

Joe Tirone had introduced the idea of a buyout to his neighbors a few days after Hurricane Sandy. About 200 dazed people were milling around the St Charles School auditorium. After he explained how the buyout would work he asked how many people would be in favor. Everyone in the room raised their hands. It was surprising but understandable.

They had suffered a decisive defeat. Almost everyone in the room had lost their homes. Plus, they had been through this many times before. Their neighborhood had a long history of being devastated by the ocean storms and scrub oak forest fires.

In 1992 a Northeaster had flooded most of these same homes, and afterwards the Oakwood Beach neighborhood had banded together to try to get permission to build a berm to protect their community.

It had taken eight years, but the group finally received permission to build the berm. But like all the other solutions it had not worked. Nobody harbored any false illusions that any kind of hard engineering solution would save their neighborhood this time either. Joe Monte said it best, "Mother Nature has taken my home back. It should not have been there from the beginning".

All the organizing they had done after the 1992 storm paid off after Hurricane Sandy. The group had stayed together and was first in line and organized when FEMA came to town to explain its experimental buyout programs.

Joe formed the Oakwood Beach Buyout Committee that night and it eventually caught the eye of Governor Cuomo who visited the area in 2013 to announce that the state would pay 100% of the pre-storm value of 141 houses and 5% more if the homeowners decided to stay on Staten Island, plus a 10% bonus to people who agreed to leave homes in areas designated as being highly vulnerable to further flooding.

It couldn't have been a more generous program, but that was not to say that it wasn't going to be difficult to move. Even though Patty Snyder's brother had drowned in the storm, she had lived in Oakwood Beach all her life.

"When we found Leonard's body after the storm, I knew that we could never go back. The buyout program is the only real solution for the area. You see, we always knew in our hearts that we were going to be in harm's way.... No one should live out there."

Chapter 15
Sandy Hook
June 25, 2016

Sandy Hook, Officers Row

For the ocean leg of my trip I joined my friend marine biologist Don Cheney on his motor cruiser, *The Smitten*, to head down the coast to see how New Jersey was recovering from the effects of Hurricane Sandy. We left New York Harbor on Saturday morning June 25, 2016.

It was flat calm as we cruised past Ellis Island and a coast guard cutter protecting the Statue of Liberty. A dozen tankers were at anchor. The value of their cargo had just plummeted in the wake of the Brexit vote. If the tankers waited a few days the price might rise and their profits could increase by tens of thousands of dollars again.

The vote also explained why there were so many young stockbrokers at last night's bar. They were blowing off steam after a day spent selling off rapidly declining stocks. It gave us a first hand view of the far ranging effects of Great Britain's momentous vote. The Brits. You've got to love them. But sometimes they act like they are stuck in a Gilbert and Sullivan show.

Later, at the swanky yacht club where we were staying, a hedge fund manager told me that oil shippers were now buying extra tankers so they could buy cheap oil from the Middle East, hold it in floating storage tankers while waiting for prices to rise and still have enough ships to deliver enough oil to maintain their cash flow.

But soon we were under the Verrazano Narrows Bridge and into the busy Ambrose Channel. On our left was Breezy Point where a gas main had exploded during Hurricane Sandy creating a post apocalyptic hell of flooded homes and greasy fires – fires that covered several blocks and left more than two hundred people homeless.

As we cruised into the lee of Sandy Hook we entered a different world. The blue square sails of bull rakers appeared on the horizon. The watermen used the sails to pull their boats over the flats while the rakers scratched the bottom for clams.

It was a back breaking but honest way to make a living, if you could still afford to live in the traditional blue-collar sections of nearby Atlantic Highlands. But that had become much more difficult after hurricane Sandy.

We could see why as we approached the Highlands. Route 36 bifurcates the small city of Atlantic Highlands. Almost all of the hurricane-damaged houses had been located along the low-lying east side of Highway, in an area called the Flats.

After the storm, there had been talk of moving the Flats buildings across the highway to the Highlands. It would have made a lot of long-term sense.

Chapter 15
Sandy Hook

Instead, the city opted for a short-term solution. They built large new homes on pilings behind a massive steel bulkhead that held back eleven feet of fill. They had essentially raised the Flats eleven feet in the air. But who could afford such homes? Certainly not watermen. It was a kind of post storm gentrification that we would see time and again as we cruised down the coast.

Tim Dillingham from the American Littoral Society drove us over the Sea Bright Bridge where we met Pete McCarthy superintendent of the Sandy Hook Unit of the Gateway National Recreational Area. Gateway includes many of the areas we had cruised past in both New York and New Jersey.

The park had been cobbled together from mostly unwanted parcels owned by the Army, the Navy, the Coast Guard, as well as city and state parks. It included all of Jamaica Bay in Brooklyn, Breezy Point in Queens and Fort Wadsworth under the Verrazano Narrows Bridge on Staten Island. Its equivalent would be the Golden Gate Recreational Area in San Francisco.

But Gateway's biggest unit was New Jersey's 12-mile long barrier spit called Sandy Hook, which had grown a mile closer to New York since the late 1800's. At one point over 10,000 soldiers and officers were stationed at Sandy Hook's Fort Hancock where they manned a series of gun batteries that protected the entrance to New York harbor.

The officers lived along Officers' Row, a neighborhood of stately 19th Century homes. One of them housed Tim's office at the headquarters of our host, the American Littoral Society. The unit also contained the oldest continually operating lighthouse in the United States, a former Nike missile site and a variegated landscape of marshes, beaches and ponds that attracts over 300 species of birds.

The Sandy Hook unit now has over 200 employees and services over 400,000 people. The Gateway Park itself serves over 4 million people a year, making it one of the most visited parks in the country.

All of Sandy Hook's lands, beaches and buildings are presided over by Pete McCarthy, a long time veteran of the park service who takes great pride in the diversity of people who use the park for swimming, fishing and bird watching. His former posting included the Statue of Liberty and New York's former slave graveyard.

Pete met us in what he calls "the park's lucky truck". It was their only vehicle that made it through the hurricane. It survived only because it had been up on a lift in the shop during the storm. Even so, water had come halfway up its hubcaps.

The day before the hurricane arrived, Pete decided he had to close the park and evacuate all his resident staff. It was a fortunate decision. We stopped at the park's entrance building. There was no water in sight on either side of the spit that was over a mile wide. But he pointed to a water line that was over 5 feet high on the side of the building. It was a chilling reminder that almost the entire spit had been under flowing oceanic water. Few would have survived if they had remained on the peninsula.

Waves left 8 to 9 feet of sand in all the parking lots, maintenance buildings and restaurants, and most of the dorms and houses had been severely damaged. It was several days before anyone was able to make it back to the park. The Navy used amphibious landing craft to check on their property and Pete set up headquarters on the bridge leading back to the mainland. It took several months for the park's workers to be able to trickle back to their jobs; many had lost their own homes.

After the workers had a chance to evaluate the damage, Gateway held a meeting to decide when to reopen. Pete told his boss he was aiming for Memorial Day weekend:

Chapter 15
Sandy Hook

"Make it May 1st."

Pete looked around the room at the people who had already worked so hard and finally shrugged.

"Ok, we'll give it a shot."

It meant repairing the army's former hundred-year-old water and sewer system and replacing many of the former concession stands with mobile food trucks. They discovered the trucks worked just as well and could be easily evacuated in the event of another storm.

Our overall impression was that Pete's park rangers, working with first responders, the Army Corps of Engineers, the Navy, Coast Guard and state officials had accomplished a Herculean task under emergency conditions to get the park up and running again. The results were impressive. The day we visited all of the park's 5,000 parking spaces were already full. It was the earliest day in the summer that this had ever happened.

Thousands of people from New York and New Jersey's urban areas had set up shop for a day of fishing, swimming and picnicking on a beautiful stretch of ocean beaches, dunes, marshes and fresh water ponds that looked more like Cape Cod or the Outer Banks than what you would expect only twenty miles from downtown Manhattan.

Chapter 16
Bay Head, New Jersey
June 26, 2016

Dredging sand to renourish New Jersey's beaches

On June 26, Don and I headed around Sandy Hook and into the oily swells of the open Atlantic. They were just enough to make us both slightly queasy but they also allowed us to see how the construction of New Jersey's artificial sand dunes was proceeding.

Some communities already had well built dunes covered with newly planted dune grass. A barge sitting almost half a mile offshore was pumping sand through pipes and spraying it onto the beach to be fashioned into an artificial sand dune near the Shark River Inlet.

Most of New Jersey's iconic boardwalks had been repaired and throngs of people were enjoying the new sand. But would this almost hundred mile long, 22-foot high sand dune be enough to save New Jersey when it was finally completed in 2017?

We reached Manasquan, the northern entrance to the Intracoastal Waterway, near high tide. The inlet was a maze of small and large boats, including one in tow behind a tugboat, just to keep us on our toes.

All the boats had to circle around each other in a tiny cramped harbor while we waited for the noon train bridge to rise. Afterwards a long procession of boats and jet skies traversed the channel until a few foolhardy souls like us turned south down the Point Pleasant Canal.

There was just enough room for two boats to pass amidships, and each boat set up waves that amplified as they ricocheted off the steel bulkheads that lined the two-mile long canal. I'm sure the canal provides endless entertainment to the occupants of the many houses along its banks.

Our cruising guide breezily acknowledged the 3 knot currents, heavy boat traffic, 2 lift bridges, waves, wakes and 6 foot depths that could be lower when the wind blew from the wrong direction. It closed with a characteristic boating understatement, "such conditions will require a little extra caution by the captains." It said nothing about the mate whose eyes never left the Fathometer. Our boat only drew 4 feet.

Prior to Hurricane Sandy we could have stayed offshore, but the storm had created so many new offshore shoals that it was deemed safer to stake your life on being able to transit the shallow canal — before the tide turned and you ran out of water. Just to add a little spice to the adventure, a dredge was stationed half way through the canal still cleaning up from the results of the storm that had shoaled up these waters four years before.

Chapter 16
Bay Head, New Jersey

But eventually we emerged from the canal into Bay Head, which had just been a marshy cul de sac at the head of Barnegat Bay before the canal was completed in 1929.

Our destination was the venerable Bay Head Yacht Club that dated back to 1888. The club owned land around most of the upper marsh area and kids were sailing a colorful fleet of Sandpipers, small shallow draft catboats made in Massachusetts. I felt like I was back in my hometown on Cape Cod.

The first thing the dockmaster told us is that Bay Head had been the epicenter of the hurricane. It seemed to be a common theme up and down the coast. He told us he and his girlfriend had spent the night on his catboat that had risen up and down on the storm surges that sloshed back and forth in the middle of the bay. But they had survived.

The rest of the residents of Bay Head had mostly evacuated and returned a few days later to a post-apocalyptic world of martial law, check points and national guardsmen standing around oil barrels filled with smoky fires. Residents felt like wartime refugees. For a month and a half you could only take two suitcases worth of belongings a day from the remains of your house.

One of the yacht club's boat detailers was able to get into the cordoned off area by crawling under a rickety pile of boats jumbled like matchsticks on top of each other. When she arrived at what was left of the yacht club where she had worked since a kid, she cried for half an hour.

But four years later you had to look hard to see damage in the village itself. It still had the feel of a quaint Cape Cod village with quiet streets lined with cedar, scraggly pine and hydrangea bushes.

The town's boardwalk had been destroyed by a storm in the Nineties and the town fathers had decided to just leave it that way, a quaint town dominated by the old money yacht club. Our detailer friend described it as a town of the newly wed and the nearly dead.

But when the state came through, asking everyone to sign easements so the Army Corps of Engineers could build this section of the sand dune to the required 22 feet, several of Bay Head's residents refused to sign, saying they didn't want a two story high sand dune blocking their ocean view. Governor Christie responded in kind.

"Residents refused to sign the easement because they didn't want a sand dune to block their view? Well now they don't have to worry about it, they got no house. So you got no house, you don't have to worry about no view."

But the beach was a revelation. Each side street that opened onto the beach had a pleasant college student who explained that you needed a badge to get onto the beach. The badges were $8 for the day and $80 for the season. You could not bring food or drinks on the beach, which took care of the messy problem of overflowing trashcans.

The badge meister let me walk down the beach to see that each side street that abutted the beach was manned by a similar college student and had two lifeguards and an antique looking rescue boat iconic to the Jersey Shore. The Bay Head Improvement Association had operated the beach this way since the year after the yacht club had been founded in 1888.

Most of the town's damaged houses had been raised on low pilings with FEMA money or at the homeowner's own expense, but there were also several empty ocean lots that nobody seemed to be in a great rush to buy or sell. The empty lots had been planted with beach grass and had undoubtedly raised the land values of the neighboring beach houses that now enjoyed an ocean view.

Chapter 16
Bay Head, New Jersey

But it was the yacht club itself that provided the most valuable post Sandy lesson. Prior to the storm the clubhouse had been a more modest building. But its planning committee had big plans and its capital committee had big bucks. When the storm destroyed the old building, the club had the cash in hand to build the much larger building.

It was a pattern we would see repeated up and down the coast. People who had their own resources could act quickly to buy out the less fortunate and build bigger and more expensive homes. The towns would be back on their feet, but what would happen during the next storm? We would find out as we continued south.

Chapter 17
The Longest Night
Lavallette, New Jersey
October 29, 2012

The Longest Night, Chris Raia show Hurricane Sandy bursting through the dunes

Chris Raia from the Tom's River police department drove Don Cheney and I south to Lavalette New Jersey where he had spent the night trapped on the island during Hurricane Sandy. This is his story of that fateful night:

Chris Raia didn't expect any problems when he started his afternoon shift on October 28. Hurricane Sandy was still several hundred miles offshore and the weathermen couldn't agree where it was going to make landfall.

But the wind was already gusty. And the ocean was gray and angry at Ortley Beach. Not much was happening, so Chris decided to go out onto the Fiedler Avenue lifeguard station. He yelled back at his partner.

"I don't think these dunes are going to hold up. The waves are already pounding them. What the hell we've got the time, I think I'll shoot some video."

Little did Officer Raia and his partner know that their video would document the last time anyone was in that lifeguard building.

1:30pm, October 29: During line-up the next day the desk sergeant assigned two policemen to each of the department's 4X4 vehicles and sent them out to patrol the township's most threatened areas. Like most communities on Barnegat Bay, Toms River was vulnerable on all four sides, its barrier beaches, the river and the bay from both north and south.

"Raia take the Ford Expedition and cover the beaches."

The assignment made sense. Chris had grown up on the township's beaches. He had met his wife at his uncle's Ortley Beach home, and he knew just how to handle the Staten Island wise guys who drove to the shore every weekend.

They lived with their parents so they could afford to lease Mercedes Benzes and take Ecstasy in the beachside nightclubs. The wise guys just laughed when you wrote them up a $40 ticket. It was just cheap parking for a night of expensive drugs.

2:30pm: The team responded to a fire on Grover Road. There was nothing they could do. The house was already engulfed in flames fanned by the wind, which was now blowing rain straight in off the ocean.

At 3:00pm they cruised past Pelican Island where all the water was out of the bay.

"Never seen that before."

Chapter 17
The Longest Night Lavallette, New Jersey

"Can't be good, that's for sure."

The storm's low-pressure area had sucked the water from the bay to form a dome of water called a storm surge, the most deadly part of a hurricane. Like the extreme low tide before a tsunami. They should have left the area immediately.

But, at 3:05pm they were sent to relieve another officer back on Ocean Ave and Fiedler. He was guarding a downed live wire. Sparks were spewing all over the glistening wet pavement.

"We shouldn't be out here!"

"Damn straight."

Just when they were wondering what else could go wrong they heard three loud booms and looked back. The ocean had just burst through the sand dunes under the boardwalk. Waves were rushing toward the sparking wire. They got out of there quickly.

The same situation held true all the way west of Route 35. The streets were covered with 6 inches of water rushing rapidly toward the center of the island from the bay. In places the ocean water and bay water had already met.

By 4:30pm the two realized they couldn't get off the island the way they had come. There was already 2 to 3 feet of water near the bridge.

They turned back north and see if they could get over the Mantoloking Bridge. There was already so much water in the road that they had to drive in the southbound lane heading north. They looked over at the bay and it was so low that large boats were heeled over in the mud.

Low pressure under the approaching storm had sucked the water out of the bay. But it would return in spades when the storm surge arrived around 8pm.

"Dispatch, ah this is officer Raia. We're going to attempt to leave the island over Mantoloking, over."

"Negative that Chris. Captain says you have to go back to Lavallette and pick up a victim and his dog and meet up with the other officers at the Lavallette Fire Station."

Chris and his partner looked at each other. It was becoming clear that they might not get off the island at all that night.

They picked up the man and his dog and sped back north, only to find whitecaps scudding straight off the ocean onto the entrance of the Mantoloking bridge. Trees and large appliances covered the road. They turned around and headed back south.

"Damn!"

By 5:15pm they were back where they had watched the water from the ocean meet the water from the bay in the middle of Rte. 35. Only now it was another foot higher.

They plowed through the water realizing that they had no other choice but to head back to the Lavallette Fire Station where several other fire, first aid and police officers were holed up with a small host of rescued civilians.

At 5:20pm they arrived at the station and told the other officers what they had just witnessed. The reality finally sunk in, they were officially stranded.

Chapter 17
The Longest Night Lavallette, New Jersey

The team inventoried their resources. They had a boat; some 4x4 vehicles and most importantly they had food, toiletries and blankets. Since the fire department had a generator the Lavallette Office of Emergency Management decided they should spend the night in the station. But Hurricane Sandy had other plans.

At 7:00pm Chris noticed water running down the street from the ocean, so his partner moved their Expedition to the station's rear parking lot. It was a little higher than the lot in front. But when he returned he noticed water entering the front door of the building. What began as a slow flow picked up pace and began flooding the building's three parking bays.

Everyone sprang into action. Now they had to move 7 civilians and eight police and firemen across the parking lot to the first aid building. Chris grabbed extra radio batteries out of the charging bank and stuffed rolls of toilet paper into trash bags. The first aid building already had food, blankets and a generator.

Firemen transported the civilians through the quickly rising water in their diesel Explorer but the first aid building was only a foot higher than the fire station.

Chris and his partner argued that they should move everyone to the two story brick school building two blocks away. It was much higher plus it had bathrooms and plenty of rooms where people could be comfortable for the long cold night ahead. But the Office of Emergency Management was more concerned about having power and since the building was their turf, they called the shots.

Half an hour later, everyone was huddled in the first aid building and the firemen were cooking hamburgers. It was almost fun. They expected that once the full moon surge passed through about 8pm, it would all be over. They were wrong.

Around 8:30pm someone looked out the window and noticed that the park bench they had been using as a marker was becoming visible again. Everyone gave a sigh of relief and Chris called his wife Nichole to tell her the worst was over. They would be fine. But it was a quick call. He still had to save power.

The officers made everyone as comfortable as possible and kept an eye on the elderly man with Alzheimer's. He kept getting up to go home. It was a bit of a trial, but their bigger concern was feeling so helpless.

Many people had not heeded their warnings to evacuate the island and were now calling in for help. They could see the orange glow of about a hundred bungalows burning in Camp Osborn, which had once been a tent site for revivalists. But there was nothing the officers could do about the multiple emergencies except listen to the dispatcher trying to talk the civilians down off the cliff.

It was the first time in his career that Chris had felt so helpless. He had been trained to help no matter what. It was also a little irritating how jazzed the firemen were. They wanted to stay up all night but Chris and his partner had switched into survival mode. They knew they needed to conserve themselves for the long haul.

At 10:30pm one of the officers pointed out the window.

"That damn bench is going under again."

"What?"

"Shoot!"

There was some concern but everyone figured the water would not reach the level it had several hours before.

Chapter 17
The Longest Night Lavallette, New Jersey

The storm surge had filled up the river and marshes and after the storm passed the water had come rushing back down into the bay again. It was like coffee sloshing back and forth in your cup of Joe in a phenomenon that oceanographers call a seiche.

The tide gauge on Mantoloking Bridge would have shown the seiche sloshing back and forth several times if it hadn't been lost along with the bridge earlier that night.

At 1:30am the rising water killed their generator.

Chris and his partner were furious. The generator was the main reason they were trapped in this single story building and now it too was kaput.

They sandbagged the doors and prayed things wouldn't get any worse.

By 2:30am they noticed that the water was starting to subside and they were safe again. As he had done all night long, Chris simply posted on facebook, "Still here." He still had to save power to the very end. His friends responded that they and his family had prayed for him all night long.

It started to get light at 6:00am and they could finally see the devastation outside. Chris had not expected it to be so bad. The building was still surrounded with two to three feet of water for as far as they could see.

Chris was finally able to call Nichole. He tried to brush things off by saying that everything was fine, but it really wasn't. Sure they had made it through the night but now what? How the hell were they going to get off this damn island?

The dispatcher called to say that the department had sent out a 5- ton military truck to get them the night before but it had been tossed around like a toy. Now the department was contacting New Jersey's State

Police marine troopers to see if they could get a boat to take them off, but it could take hours because there was so much debris in the water.

At 12:30 that afternoon, the police boat finally arrived. It powered through the playground, over the roadway and right up to their building still in two feet of water.

But they had a new problem. The elderly man with Alzheimer's had gone into diabetic shock. The dispatcher told Chris they would have a medical team waiting for them on the mainland.

The team left the building at 1:30pm keeping a close eye on the victim as the boat made its way to Cranberry Bay Marina where a NJ State military truck met them and transferred the semi-conscious gentleman to one of the only mainland hospitals that was still in operation.

At 2:05pm the truck returned and the survivors climbed in and headed through a bleak scene. Pelican Island was almost completely underwater. Cars, jet skies and pieces of buildings littered the streets and all the telephone poles were down, Tangles of mostly dead wire were everywhere.

At 2:10pm the survivors climbed down off the truck on the west side of Tunney Bridge where they were welcomed by their co-workers and friends. Most of them were also in the emergency services and knew what Chris and the other officers had been through.

The captain who had told them to stay on the island almost two days before gave them a long emotional hug. He had not slept all night waiting to hear if two of his best officers had made it back alive. They were finally home.

Chapter 18
Recover or Retreat?
Tom's River, NJ
June 27, 2016

Tom's River, Homes built on the same footprint as before Hurricane Sandy. A more expensive disaster waiting to happen

On June 27, Don Cheney and I joined Chris Raia to retrace his footsteps the night of Hurricane Sandy. It would also allow us to see how, or if, New Jersey's barrier beach communities had recovered from the storm.

Although recently retired, Chris is still a young but seasoned cop. The kind you would feel comfortable with in any kind of emergency. He would probably even crack a few jokes while saving your life.

Chris picked us up in Bay Head and, like everyone else, explained that now we were going to see the true epicenter of the storm. Don and I smiled at each other. This had become a familiar refrain.

Also like everyone else, Chris had a set of pictures he kept on his tablet. It was almost like people were still haunted by the storm and needed the photographs to remind them they had really survived such complete devastation.

As we drove toward Tom's River we started to see more and more damaged and missing homes. Nearly half of New Jersey's $3.4 Billion ratable losses had occurred in this single township. Parts of it still looked like a ghost town four years later. This truly was the epicenter of the storm.

We discussed a recent Frontline Program on PBS that explained that thousands of Sandy survivors had not received any money from the Federal Flood Insurance Program, so they were still paying rent, plus a mortgage and insurance on houses that they couldn't live in.

Although it is a federal agency, the Flood Insurance Program is now run by private insurance companies under contract to the government. After the hurricane, the companies hired hundreds of adjusters to handle the myriads of claims. The adjusters followed the procedures and determined that almost all of the people who applied had suffered damage and should receive settlements.

But when the managers of the program realized how much money they stood to lose, they reviewed the claims, so that thousands of people lost their formerly promised settlements. The managers had determined that hairline cracks in the claimants' basements were caused by land movements prior to the storm.

Isn't that convenient? How many houses built on sand wont have hairline cracks from land movement? For this the private companies were paid a 30 percent profit from the non-profit public agency?

Chapter 18
Recover or Retreat? Tom's River, NJ

One of the first places we stopped was the iconic Mantoloking Bridge. I had seen dozens of photographs showing where the ocean had blasted through the island washing out the bridge and scores of homes.

All of Mantoloking's 521 barrier beach homes had been damaged, which had destroyed a third of the borough's tax base, the most of any municipality in New Jersey.

But by 2016, most of Mantoloking's homes had been replaced. Chris explained that they were owned by people who had either been able to sell their lots right away or had their own resources to rebuild before they received their FEMA checks. Like the Bay Head Yacht Club, all of these new houses were larger and more costly than before.

He also explained that state officials had rushed to refill all of the inlets that had been punched through the beaches into Barnegat Bay. But if officials had kept the inlets open and built bridges over them instead, they could have revived Barnegat Bay from its chronic problems with eutrophication caused by septic tanks leaching into the bay. New York officials had discovered how to inexpensively address this problem after Sandy had broken through Fire Island.

As we continued south we started to see the prototypical Jersey Shore. People sat outside modest bungalows talking to their neighbors across narrow streets made of crystal white sand.

But their homes were interspersed with abandoned houses overgrown with weeds and emanating moldy odors. Some of the small houses were being raised so high on pilings that their owners were installing costly elevators.

Chris also showed us several acres of burned out lots in the old Osborne revival camp in Brick Township. He explained that he and his fellow officers had seen the glow of them burning the night they had been trapped in the Lavallette Fire Station.

Over a hundred 1920's era bungalows had burned to the ground after the storm burst through a gas main. Many of the residents who had lived in the tightknit neighborhood for decades were still displaced. But architects had drawn up plans for a 90-unit condo complex that would be way out of reach for the former residents, yet another case of post storm gentrification.

And what was supposed to protect all these new larger homes? A 22 foot high sand dune that will run the length of New Jersey when it is completed by 2017. But would it just be a hundred mile long security blanket offering only the illusion of safety?

I was reminded of the 40-foot high sand dune that Plum Island homeowners threw up in front of their homes the night before Hurricane Sandy. The following morning people stared in awe at the owner's stairs hanging in the air 40 feet above the beach. The 40 foot high sand dune had been washed entirely away during a single tidal cycle.

If another Sandy occurred next week, it was clear that the losses would not be $16 Billion, but closer to $32 Billion. And most of the damage would happen on the string of barrier islands that fringe the East Coast.

But that is not the only problem. Earlier in the summer 19 prominent scientists, lead by Jim Hansen, released a peer-reviewed paper that predicted that sea levels would rise by 9 feet in the next 50 years and about 3 feet in the next 20 years.

As if that weren't enough, in the Seventies scientists had figured out that when the rate of sea level rise rises above 3 feet every century, barrier beaches will start to break apart.

So if Hansen's paper is as prescient as all his previous papers, it really doesn't matter what we do. No amount of hard or soft engineering solutions will be able to save barrier islands and the communities they harbor.

Chapter 18
Recover or Retreat? Tom's River, NJ

Instead of blindly rebuilding barrier beaches devastated by such storms shouldn't we be using each storm as an opportunity to gradually retreat from these dubious redoubts?

Chapter 19
Oregon Inlet
North Carolina
2017

Oregon Inlet and Bonner Bridge. Courtesy Great Lakes Dredging

When you push down from Virginia into North Carolina you are in the realm of the fabled Outer Banks. From here south to Cape Lookout, the islands are long and narrow, the estuaries are as wide as 30 miles and the inlets are few and far between.

The first inlet you run into is actually the remains of the Old Currituck Inlet that closed between 1811 and 1829. As soon as the inlet closed, the sound started to freshen, making it a favorite spot for hunting and fishing for freshwater species. But now there is a move afoot to build an artificial inlet, to bring back saltwater gamefish.

The next true inlet you encounter presents a far more complicated story—a story that has important implications for people who live on places like Plum Island.

In 1846, a hurricane burst through the Outer Banks creating the Oregon Inlet, with Bodie Island to the North and Pea Island to the south. It must have been quite a storm because it also opened up the Outer Bank' other major inlet, Ocracoke as well as the Old Harbor Life Savings Station Inlet off Chatham, Massachusetts.

The Oregon Inlet received its curious name from the first ship to transit the inlet after riding out the storm in Pamlico Sound. But immediately after opening, the inlet started migrating south, devouring Pea Island and allowing Bodie Island to regrow in a shoally sort of way. Since forming, the inlet has migrated 2 miles south at the average rate of 66 feet a year, causing the Coast Guard to move its station four times.

As soon as the inlet opened it became a boon and a problem, providing a new inlet, through shoaling, for fishing boats but isolating Hatteras Island. Fishermen proposed solving the first problem by dredging the inlet. But the proposal died on the vine as fishermen learned how to navigate the area. The second problem would be solved first by ferries, then by building the flood prone Bonner Bridge.

But by 1946, the inlet had shoaled so much that trawlers and menhaden boats had to steam to Hampton Roads Virginia to offload their valuable catches. So fishermen requested that the government dredge the channel to a 14 foot depth and build two jetties to stabilize the inlet in place.

The U.S. Congress authorized building jetties in 1970. But by that time the Department of the Interior was involved because it owned both the Cape Hatteras National Seashore and the Pea Island National Wildlife Refuge. The department asked Douglas Inman from the Scripps Institute of Oceanography to chair a panel of scientists and engineers from the American Academy of Sciences and the American Academy of Engineers to evaluate the Army Corps of Engineer's proposal. The panel of prestigious scientists from outside North Carolina found

Chapter 19
Oregon Inlet North Carolina

numerous shortcomings in the Corps' proposal that have never been fully addressed to this day.

The panel pointed out that the inlet would cut off the supply of sand flowing to Pea Island and doubted the viability of the Corp's proposal to build an untested, sloped front, floating breakwater so that sand could bypass the inlet. They also noted that the jetties would prevent larval marine fish from entering the Sound to grow into maturity and that increasing charter boats' access to the Gulf Stream fishery would only put more pressure on an already declining resource.

Most of all, the panel pointed out that it would be far cheaper to just continue dredging the inlet on a regular basis without risking all the unintended consequences that could occur from interfering with such a dynamic oceanic system. They were opposed by the Oregon Inlet User's Association and supported by the Southern Environmental Legal Foundation.

The biggest difference between the Oregon Inlet situation and the situation on Plum Island is that the residents of Plum Island's Northern Reservation Terrace were taken by surprise, because no adequate science had been done. They didn't expect that repairing the Merrimack River's South Jetty would jeopardize their homes. Otherwise they might have brought in a powerful environmental group like the Conservation Law Foundation to argue against what turned into a $24 million dollar mistake.

Chapter 20
New Shelly Island
Cape Hatteras, NC
2017

North of Cape Lookout the string of long, narrow barrier islands have evocative names like Duck, Kill Devil Hills and Nags Head. The latter was named because a horse supposedly caught her neck in the crotch of a tree, and sailors could see the horse's white skull gleaming in the tree for years after the event.

As we have seen, the northern islands have been breached by four main inlets that tend to open and reopen opposite the four main rivers that deliver millions of gallons of rich black organic water into these productive sounds. The flooded shores are lined with fresh water loving cypress, graceful tupelo and hardy swamp maple trees.

South of Cape Lookout, the islands are short and stubby and separated from the mainland by as many as 19 ever changing inlets that keep the water brackish and vegetation to low salt tolerant marsh grass species.

But during the summer of 2017, all eyes were on the center of the Outer Banks, where a new mile-long, three-football field wide island had suddenly emerged out of the ocean off Cape Hatteras. It was only 50 yards offshore in water that was just 5 feet deep so people could paddle across the narrow isthmus despite the many sharks and rays the size of barn doors that abounded in the area.

The son of one of the first reporters to visit the new caprice of geology dubbed it Shelly Island and the name stuck. But it turned out the island contained considerably more than shells. People kept finding whalebones and pieces of old shipwrecks jutting out of the sand and on July 14 the beach had to be evacuated because two unexploded bombs were found lying on the strand.

It was almost as if the ocean had dug up a graveyard and piled up all the remains on this mile long heap of sand. In fact this was largely what had happened.

Cape Hatteras is familiar to New Englanders because almost all our Northeasters and most of our hurricanes clip "Cape Hat" before slamming into Cape Cod. This is because Cape Hatteras juts so far out into Hurricane Alley, the main thoroughfare for Northeasters and hurricanes barreling north.

South of Hatteras the warm waters of the Gulf Stream caress the Carolina coast giving it, its warm tropical feel. Her shores are graced with southern vegetation and pelicans glide silently over lines of waves just offshore.

But Cape Hatteras is also where the warm waters of the Gulf Stream clash with the cold waters of the Labrador Current before swerving out to sea. There they work with each other to create the turbulence and treacherous waters of Diamond Shoals, the notorious graveyard of the Atlantic. But the currents also collude to push underwater shoals of sand together until they emerge above the surface as dry shoals like Shelly Island.

The same thing happened at the end of the Ice Ages when the seas were rising and the waves, wind and currents worked together to create the Outer Banks which were also slowly moving shoreward as the seas rose. It is worth noting that barrier beaches are artifacts of rising seas. If our planet started cooling or, God forbid, our seas stopped rising, barrier beaches would stop growing and end up being sandy ridges abandoned on upland areas.

Of course at the end of the Ice Ages, nobody really cared about who owned all the new islands being formed. Herds of woolly mammoth just moved back from the coast that was retreating as much as 60 feet a year, and hoped they wouldn't encounter any of the new two-footed creatures so intent on driving them into extinction.

Chapter 20
New Shelly Island Cape Hatteras, NC

Today these same disputatious bipedals are firmly in charge and the first thing on our minds is who should own such a valuable piece of new real estate. The State of North Carolina insists that Shelly Island is theirs because it still lies in her state waters. But the superintendent of the Cape Hatteras National Seashore points out that the isthmus between Shelly Island and the Seashore is only 50 yards wide and, as soon it closes, the island will fall under his jurisdiction.

Chapter 21
Daufuskie Island
South Carolina
July 13, 2017

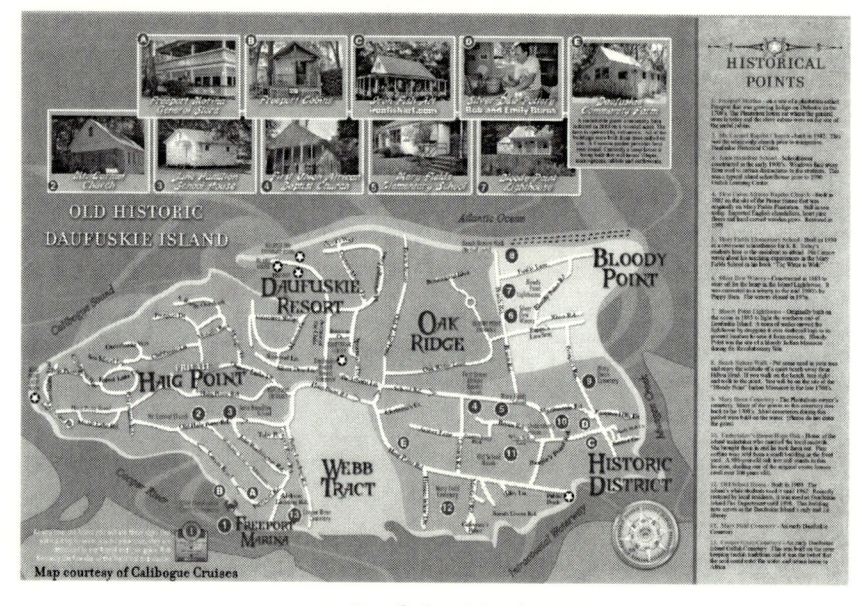

Daufuskie Island

On July 13, the Wall Street Journal inadvertently signaled the vulnerability of the high-end waterfront homes that their real estate section depends on for advertising revenue.

It was an article about South Carolina's Daufuskie Island – an island that is laid out like a well-designed experiment.

The Haig Point resort lies on the north end of the island. Its residents pay a $20,000 initiation fee, a $23,000 fee to use the golf course, equestrian facilities, and country club on top of waterfront homes that cost up to

$2.85 Million dollars. About 265 homes in the gated community are occupied.

The decaying remains of the Melrose Resort lie in the middle of the island. The clubhouse is closed, the golf course is overgrown with weeds and its beach cottages are abandoned. Only 17 families still live within the former resort.

Bloody Point sits on the south end of the island. It is still open, but its present owner is trying to sell the resort. Only five of its homes are occupied.

The only part of the island that can be considered balanced and thriving is the former Gullah settlement, which has been turned into a historic district. Its occupants cater to the whims of the wealthy residents, offering them a funky restaurant, coffee shops and boat transportation to the island that allows no cars, as well as eco tours for day-trippers and renters.

This being the Wall Street Journal, the article concentrated on economics and blamed the problems of the island on the 2008 real estate collapse.

What the article didn't show was that many of the waterfront homes had large unsightly plastic sandbags in front of them, for Daufuskie like so many other East Coast islands is being slowly but inexorably consumed by sea level rise.

This explains in a more fundamental way why only Haig's Point prospers. It is the only place on the island where residents can purchase federal flood insurance.

Chapter 21
Daufuskie Island South Carolina

South Carolina would like to expand the covered area, but the program is $24 billion dollars in debt and due to be discontinued in September 2017. It is doubtful that the dysfunctional Trump administration, or the dead in the water Congress, will be in any kind of position to fix it.

The article inadvertently made another point. Barrier beaches are not really very good places to own a house but they are excellent places to rent. This might be the future of islands like Daufuskie.

Chapter 22
Cayo Costa, Florida
February 21, 2017

Cayo Costa

By mid-February I was weary of New England's northeasters, so I decided to fly south to see how Florida would fare in our present era of rising seas and stronger storms. My informant for these explorations would be John Martin, an old friend from high school who now lives in Punta Gorda, near Fort Meyers.

Our trip started out on Cayo Costa, a barrier beach island on Florida's West Coast. My family has a longstanding relationship with this island. My father brought me to the island thirty years before, and when we found the scale of a tarpon with his father's initials on it in a nearby bar he remembered the day my grandfather had caught it. Not because of the fish. But because my grandmother had so ticked at my grandfather for returning home several sheets to windward after celebrating all day on Useppa Island. Those were in the days when you went down to Boca

Grande by train and stayed for the full season at the gracious Gasparilla Inn.

Unlike nearby Sanibel and Captiva islands, no bridge or revetments had ever been built on Cayo Costa. This had left the island able to fulfill its function as a natural barrier against major storms, so people could live safely behind the barrier beaches as the Callussa Indians had done hundreds of years before. The lack of houses and infrastructure made it easier for Florida to make the island into a state park in 1971.

The wisdom of that effort had been tested when Hurricane Charley arrived on August 13, 2004. After passing over Key West as a Category 3 hurricane, Charley had suddenly turned northeast and increased to a category 5 hurricane before smashing over Cayo Costa and on into Punta Gorda area, where it caused $15 billion in damages and left hundreds of people living in FEMA trailers years after the storm had passed.

But Cayo Costa looked much as I remembered it 30 years before, and probably much like it looked five hundred years before that. Tendrils of fog lifted slowly along its nine miles of powdery white beaches. However, all the Australian pine trees I remembered towering over the island had been snapped in two. Park rangers had spent years vainly trying to remove the invasive trees by chain saw, before Charley did it for them in two minutes flat.

Now copses of native sea grapes were thriving in the sunlight where the pines used to be. The wild boar that used to emerge from native Palmetto palm groves to root for mole crabs on the tidal flats, and the feral horses that used to nuzzle visiting boaters seemed to be gone. But alligators still lurked in the shallow lagoon just behind the swimming beach.

Chapter 22
Cayo Costa, Florida

And of course the productive waters of the Gulf of Mexico still produced billions of shells that washed up on the deceptively quiet beaches of Cayo Costa – deceptive because they still remained ready to absorb the powers of the next hurricane. They reflected the benefit of leaving a barrier beach in its natural state to stave off future storms. And the best way to do that was to make it into a public park.

And now the park was thriving. Every day hundreds of visitors arrived in their own boats or on small ferries to be taken across the island in modified golf carts driven by park volunteers. There, they could spread out along a seven-mile long pristine white Gulf of Mexico beach, or pitch a tent and spend a week fishing.

If you looked carefully you could see where the beach had rolled over itself as it moved inland during hurricane Charley and you could see some areas of slight erosion. But you never read anything about erosion on Cayo Costa because it had no houses or streets to wash away. So the island just remains a pristine natural barrier island, ready to protect the mainland from the next Hurricane Charlie.

We hoped to compare Cayo Costa to a built-up barrier beach on the hurricane prone Atlantic Coast of Florida. We scrutinized the map and found the perfect location 200 miles directly east. It happened to be Mar-a-Lago, President Trump's winter white house on tony Palm Beach. We wondered if they would let two old geezers from New England in. Perhaps we should mention we knew Bill Bellichick.

Chapter 23
Lake Okeechobee
February 22, 2017

Lake "O"

Sheets of rain splattered against the windshield as John and I sped across Florida. It was altogether fitting that we should arrive at Lake Okeechobee in such a storm. Most of Florida's biggest and most complicated environmental problems stem from agricultural wastes washing into Lake "O".

For thousands of years water flowed from the Orlando area south into Lake Okeechobee, then on through the Everglades to be filtered and cleansed as it seeped south toward the Florida Keys.

All this started to change with Florida's first land boom in the 1920's. Salesmen would travel by train through the mid-West extolling the Sunshine State as America's new home for year-round farming, "Why the soil is so rich you don't even have to fertilize it. No sirree just throw down some seeds and watch 'em grow." Never mind that most of the lots were underwater and would still have to be "reclaimed" from the Everglades.

The way they reclaimed farmland was to build an earthen dike to hold back Lake "O"'s waters from seeping south. The results were spectacular at first. Farm hands planted row upon row of sugarcane, citrus and vegetables in the rich, mucky black soil.

But by the summer of 1926 heavy rains had already raised the lake to the edge of the dike when the great Miami Hurricane came barreling through. A wall of water smashed through the dike, trapping hundreds of people in their beds as the lake surged through their doors and windows. In the end the Great Miami Hurricane killed 400 people and left 40,000 homeless.

After the storm, Herbert Hoover stepped in and built a new 243-mile dam that encircled the entire lake. But in 1928 the San Felipe-Okeechobee Hurricane smashed a 21-mile long hole through the dike and a 15-foot high wall of water surged down through the five towns we had just driven through. In scenes premonicient of Hurricane Katrina, people had to cut through their roofs and use the bodies of bloated dead cows as life rafts while fighting off swarms of angry, large water moccasins. The San Felipe-Okeechobee hurricane was the second most deadly hurricane in history, drowning more people than Katrina.

Today Lake "O"'s problems have become even more complex. Now they are affecting water quality on both the East and West Coasts of Florida.

When we were staying in Boca Grande, the red tide was so bad that you could tell how many people were in a house simply hearing them cough. Many elderly people had to cut their vacation short because of respiratory problems that can become fatal when aggravated by red tide aerosols. And for the past few years Florida's East Coast has

Chapter 23
Lake Okeechobee

been covered with a gross green algal mats from Stuart Florida to Palm Beach. And all these problems have their start in Lake "O".

Runoff from cattle ranches flows into the lake from the north and sugarcane fertilizers flows into the lake from the south where they mix in a petri dish the size of Delaware.

Then heavy rainfall like what we were experiencing, puts pressure on the dam so officials divert the fetid waters down the St Lucie River to Florida's east coast and down the Caloosahatchee River to Florida's west coast. There, the potent mix of nitrates and phosphates in the freshwater fertilize the saltwater dinoflagellates creating toxic red tides and putrid green algae blooms that stretch for miles.

We wondered if we would see this when we reached Mar-a-Lago. Little did we know that we would be occupied with more pressing concerns.

Chapter 24
Mar-a-Lago
February 23, 2017

Trump Door.

After visiting Cayo Costa, John had taken us by boat to Cabbage Key. Cabbage Key and its sister island, Useppa, are unique archaeological sites. Estuaries are the only ecosystems that are biologically productive enough to be able to support large year round populations of humans without resorting to agriculture.

This made life easy for the Callussa people because they didn't have to build irrigation canals or do any hard agricultural labor. But their leaders took care of that. They organized the Callussas into unpaid work gangs to build step pyramids like those built by the Mayans in Mexico. The pyramids were located on the many keys that lay protected behind the string of barrier beaches that included Sanibel, Captiva and Gasparilla Islands.

The Callusas hafted wooden handles onto the Lightning Whelks that proliferated in the area and used the heavy shells as grub hoes to build the pyramids. They used the whelks once again to cover the pyramids with abstract whorled patterns. Then they built a series of canals so their scouts could scoot from behind the barrier islands to the pyramids to warn of danger. This proved useful when Spanish explorers started snooping around their kingdom in the 1600's.

Today the remains of these step pyramids and their extensive shell middens are the highest points in Southwest Florida—all that is left of their leaders' overweening egos and taste in monuments to themselves.

We were reminded of that as we drove across Florida to visit President Trump's Mar-a-Lago on Palm Beach. My original plan was to simply take a few pictures of the Italianate villa that sits only 4 feet above sea level in our country's most hurricane prone state. But that was before anyone realized that the president intended to run his shambolic administration from his imperial looking villa all winter long.

So we didn't really know what to expect. I told John I would be more than happy if we could just take a few pictures from the car. Even if we were turned away I could probably write a story about the expensive security surrounding our president who has residences in New York, Washington, New Jersey and Florida.

We had planned to park at a nearby island and take pictures across the bayou, but the bridge to Palm Beach was open so we decided to see if we could drive by Mar-a-Lago itself.

No security was in sight so we drove down a side street where a cop car was parked. We figured we could ask if it was OK to take a few photographs but the car was empty so we parked and walked.

Chapter 24
Mar-a-Lago

The adjacent street was separated from Mar-a-Lago by a high hedge and trees, but a path led through the vegetation to an open gate. I took a few steps down the path and took a photograph of a huge American flag flapping over the red-tiled building. A couple explained that the city of Palm Beach had tried to restrict the height of the oversized flag, but had been overridden — by executive order no doubt.

Since nobody was around I took a few more steps and suddenly realized I was almost inside the compound itself. A groundskeeper eventually came along and explained that this was private resort and that we would have to leave. We said we were sorry and walked back to our car.

Nobody had bothered to ask for credentials or just what exactly we thought we were doing. Even though the President wasn't in residence we were shocked by the lack of security.

But I suppose if I were President Trump I would be far less concerned about two old geezers with cameras than section 4 of the Constitution's 25th amendment. That's the one that empowers a majority of the principal officers of the executive departments to declare the President unfit for office and to install the Vice President in his stead.

It was fascinating to see how a little short-term problem like a political scandal could draw your attention away from a long-term problem like sea level rise. I wonder if the Calussas ever noticed the same thing?

Chapter 24
Mar-a-Lago